AMAZING ANIMALS
PRONGHORN
BY CHRISTOPHER BAHN

CREATIVE EDUCATION • CREATIVE PAPERBACKS

Published by Creative Education and Creative Paperbacks
P.O. Box 227, Mankato, Minnesota 56002
Creative Education and Creative Paperbacks
are imprints of The Creative Company
www.thecreativecompany.us

Design by The Design Lab
Art direction by Graham Morgan
Edited by Jill Kalz

Images by flickr/Tom Koerner/USFWS, 17; Getty Images/ Art Wolfe, 5, FRANKHILDEBRAND, 18, greymountainphotography, 9, gsagi, 22–23, TSnowImages, 14; Pexels/Brett Sayles, 2, Dick Hoskins, 21, Ken Frank, 6; Shutterstock/Chris Desborough, cover, 1; Unsplash/Patrick Hendry, 10; Wikimedia Commons/Kenraiz, 12, Trevor Sullivan, 13, USFWS Mountain-Prairie, 20

Copyright © 2025 Creative Education, Creative Paperbacks
International copyright reserved in all countries.
No part of this book may be reproduced in any form without written permission from the publisher.

Library of Congress Cataloging-in-Publication Data
Names: Bahn, Christopher (Children's story writer), author.
Title: Pronghorn / by Christopher Bahn.
Description: Mankato, Minnesota : Creative Education and Creative Paperbacks, [2025] | Series: Amazing animals | Includes bibliographical references and index. | Audience: Ages 6–9 | Audience: Grades 2–3 | Summary: "Discover the made-for-speed pronghorn! Explore the deerlike mammal's anatomy, diet, habitat, and life cycle. Captions, on-page definitions, a Blackfeet animal folktale, additional resources, and an index support elementary-aged kids"— Provided by publisher.
Identifiers: LCCN 2024011031 (print) | LCCN 2024011032 (ebook) | ISBN 9798889892465 (library binding) | ISBN 9781682776124 (paperback) | ISBN 9798889893578 (ebook)
Subjects: LCSH: Pronghorn—Juvenile literature. | Pronghorn—Behavior—Juvenile literature. | Adaptation (Biology)—Juvenile literature.
Classification: LCC QL737.U52 B34 2025 (print) | LCC QL737.U52 (ebook) | DDC 599.63/9—dc23/eng/20240415
LC record available at https://lccn.loc.gov/2024011031
LC ebook record available at https://lccn.lo gov/2024011032

Printed in China

Table of Contents

Light and Fast	4
Home on the Grasslands	10
Herd Life	14
Tough to Catch	18
A Pronghorn Tale	22
Read More	24
Websites	24
Index	24

Although they are often called deer or antelope, pronghorn are most closely related to giraffes.

Pronghorn are deerlike **mammals**. They live in the western United States, Canada, and Mexico. Pronghorn are known for their speed. They are among the fastest animals on Earth.

mammals animals with fur or hair that give birth to live young and feed them milk

PRONGHORN

Pronghorn have tan and white fur. They have two-toed hooves and long legs. Male pronghorn have short black horns with sharp points. Animals with hooves and horns are called bovids. Cows and sheep are bovids, too.

Pronghorn don't need much water and can survive in very dry places.

Pronghorn

Pronghorn stand about 3 feet (0.9 meter) tall at the shoulder. Females weigh 70 to 100 pounds (31–45 kilograms). Males are larger, at 100 to 150 pounds (45–68 kg). In the wild, pronghorn usually live four to five years.

Pronghorn are named for the forward-facing points (prongs) on their horns.

A pronghorn's fur color helps it blend in with sandy soil and dry grasses.

Many pronghorn make their home in grasslands near the Rocky Mountains. They are very good at living on the prairie. They have adapted to cold winters and hot summers. Other pronghorn live in dry deserts.

adapted changed to improve the chances of survival

prairie a large, mostly treeless area covered by grasses and short shrubs

Sagebrush, a pronghorn favorite food

Pronghorn eat grasses and flowering plants. They eat shrubs and cacti, too. Their stomachs are tough. Pronghorn feed on 400 kinds of plants. Many of those plants would make other animals sick.

Pronghorn spend much of their day eating to keep up their energy.

13

PRONGHORN

Within days, young pronghorn can run faster than a human.

In spring, female pronghorn give birth. They usually have two babies, called fawns. Fawns camouflage themselves in the tall grass. Their mother feeds them milk. After about two weeks, mothers and fawns rejoin the main group.

camouflage to blend in with the surroundings

Pronghorn herds move hundreds of miles every year to find food and avoid snow.

In summer, pronghorn live in small groups called bands. A band has one male and a few females. In winter, pronghorn live in large herds. There may be thousands of animals in a herd. Large numbers keep pronghorn safe from **predators**.

predators animals that kill and eat other animals

The top speed of a pronghorn is 60 miles (96 kilometers) per hour. Only cheetahs run faster. But pronghorn can run for a longer time. They can run 7 miles (11 km) or more without stopping.

Pronghorn can easily zigzag on the uneven ground of the prairie.

Besides speed, pronghorn use their eyesight to keep safe. Their eyes are as big as an elephant's. Pronghorn can see danger up to 3 miles (4.8 km) away. These amazing animals are tough to catch!

Pronghorn are always on the lookout for dangers such as hungry coyotes and wolves.

21

PRONGHORN

A Pronghorn Tale

The Blackfeet

people have an old story about the pronghorn. When the god Na'pi made the pronghorn, he put it in the mountains to live. But the pronghorn stumbled on the rocky ground. It was unhappy. Na'pi realized his mistake. He moved the pronghorn to the grasslands. There it could run faster than the wind. The animal was happy and lived a good life.

Read More

Duling, Kaitlyn. *Pronghorn*. Minneapolis: Bellwether Media, 2021.

Johnson, Rebecca L. *A Walk in the Prairie*. Minneapolis: Lerner Publications, 2021.

Websites

National Geographic: Pronghorn
https://www.nationalgeographic.com/animals/mammals/facts/pronghorn
Learn all about these animals of the prairie.

National Park Service: Pronghorn
https://www.nps.gov/yell/learn/nature/pronghorn.htm
Read about the pronghorn of Yellowstone National Park.

Note: Every effort has been made to ensure that the websites listed above are suitable for children, that they have educational value, and that they contain no inappropriate material. However, because of the nature of the Internet, it is impossible to guarantee that these sites will remain active indefinitely or that their contents will not be altered.

Index

bovids, 7
dangers, 16, 20
eyes, 20
food, 12, 15, 16
fur, 7, 11
groups, 15, 16
homes, 4, 11, 22
hooves, 7
horns, 7, 8
offspring, 15
sizes, 8
speed, 4, 15, 19, 20, 22